ISBN 0 86112 695 5
Animal Life-Survival in the Wild has been published by Brimax Books as four
separate volumes – Growing Up, Living Together, Nature's Builders
and Staying Alive.
© Brimax Books Ltd 1988. All rights reserved.
Published by Brimax Books, Newmarket, England 1988
Second printing 1990
Produced by Mandarin Offset
Printed in Hong Kong

ANIMAL LIFE
SURVIVAL IN THE WILD

Written by
Karen O'Callaghan &
Kate Londesborough

BRIMAX BOOKS • NEWMARKET • ENGLAND

Artists

Bob Bampton
Jim Channell
Paula Chasty
Sue Gibson
Ian Jackson
Steve Kaye
Alan Male
Colin Newman
John Rignall

Introduction

Animal Life introduces young readers to the fascinating world of animals, covering all aspects of their lives and behaviour.
The book is divided into sections. Subjects are grouped within each section so that children can understand the similarities and differences between species. They will learn about early development, caring and co-operation, home building, finding food and how animals adapt to their environment. Survival is the key link in all these areas.

Growing Up explores birth and early life. It describes the methods parents use to feed and protect their young.

Living Together shows how animals increase their chances of survival by living together in groups where they can protect each other from danger and co-operate in finding food.

Nature's Builders demonstrates the amazing diversity of skills animals use to provide themselves and their families with a safe place in which to live.

Staying Alive describes how animals find food, which animals are hunters and what clever techniques are used by their prey to defend themselves and escape.

In the Wild covers environments. It shows how animals cope with changes in their surroundings and finally how vital it is that the natural world remains a safe place in which wild animals can live and breed in peace.

Animal Life is suitable for children of 5–10 years.
The easy-to-read text is linked with realistic illustrations and vivid photographs.

Contents

Staying Alive

In the Wild

Growing Up

Baby animals

The world is a new and very strange place for all baby animals.

turtle

orang-utan

caterpillar

swans

Some stay with their parents. Others live alone and take care of themselves. They all have a lot to learn.

Born all alone

These babies can all look after themselves as soon as they are born. Their parents do not stay with them.

Before they hatch, **snakes** grow an egg tooth. They use this sharp tooth to cut open the shell. These baby snakes will find their own food.

egg tooth

The baby **dog shark** has a yolk-sac joined to its body. The newborn shark feeds on this.

Mother **turtles** lay their eggs in the sand and leave them.

Soon the babies dig their way out and rush into the sea. This is a dangerous time for the baby **turtles**. Some of them are eaten by birds before they reach the water.

This **monarch butterfly** lays her eggs on a leaf.

The **caterpillars** will eat the leaf as soon as they are born.

Cared for at birth

When these babies are born, their parents feed them and protect them from danger.

Baby **shrews** are born in a nest made of dry grasses. When they are strong enough to leave the nest, the family all stay together.

When they are born, **kittens** have their eyes closed. After one week their eyes will open. The kittens stay close to their mother and suck her milk. They cannot look after themselves. The mother cat licks their fur to clean them.

The baby **hippopotamus** is born under the water. It learns to swim alongside its mother. It will be able to swim before it learns to walk on land. These babies live in special nursery groups with other mothers and babies.

Cichlids *(siklids)* carry their young in their mouths. They let them out to feed. If an enemy comes too close, they suck the babies in again.

Weak and strong

Some babies are born weak and helpless.
They stay with their parents for many weeks.
They need a safe home while they grow.

Song sparrows are born in a nest in the grass. At first they are blind. They have no feathers and cannot stand up or walk. Their parents bring them food.

The **macaque** does not build a nest for her baby. She keeps it warm and safe in her arms. At first, the baby is so weak that it can only cling to her and suck milk. After many weeks it will be strong enough to ride on her back.

The mother **dog** knows her puppies will be safe by her side.
If one wanders away, she carries it back by the scruff
of its neck.

Squirrels make
a nest of sticks for
their babies. They
will stay in the nest
for 8 weeks. If there
is danger, the
mother squirrel will
move her babies to
a safer place.

Other babies still need care, but are much stronger when they are born.

Mallard ducks use their nest only for a short time. When the ducklings hatch they can see and they have soft feathers. As soon as the feathers dry, they all leave the nest for water. The ducklings can swim and their mother shows them where to find their own food.

Baby **hares**, called leverets, are born with fur and their eyes are open. They can run about after only a few minutes. They drink milk from their mother at first, but will soon find small plants to eat by themselves.

The mother **reindeer** does not build a nest. Her calf is born on to the ground. The herd must keep moving to find food. After resting for two days the calf will be able to walk with them.

The young **bush-baby** is born covered with hair. After one day it can run quite fast along the branches. It sucks its mother's milk and after two weeks it will also eat soft fruit.

Where are they born?

In a tunnel

A **platypus** lays two eggs in a tunnel. At first, the babies are naked and blind.

In a fur-lined nest at the end of a tunnel these baby **rabbits** are born. They grow quickly. At two weeks old they can run.

In a cave

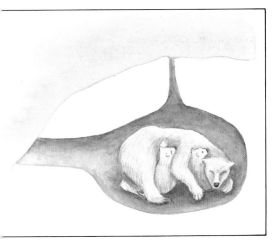

Polar bear cubs are
born deep in
a snow cave.
At birth they are very small, only 25 cms (10 inches) long,
and they are blind and deaf. They will not be able to hear
for nearly 3 months.

Under a tree

The **tiger** cubs are
hidden under
a fallen tree. When
they are born, they
are blind and very
tiny.

In a pouch

size at birth

A baby **red kangaroo** is as long as a thumb nail when it is born. It is called a joey. It lives in its mother's pouch and will climb back in even when it has grown much bigger.

Virginia opossums have 13 tiny babies. They stay in the pouch for 10 weeks. Then they are carried about by their mother.

In a tree

Sloths live high up in the trees. The baby is born upside-down and holds on to its mother's fur.

On the ice

Emperor penguins live in the snow and ice. The chick hatches during the winter. The father holds it on a fold or flap of skin, resting on his feet. This keeps the chick warm.

In the water

A baby **blue whale** is born under the water. It is born tail first so that it will not drown. As soon as its head is out, its mother nudges it up to the air to breathe. Another female swims nearby, watching out for sharks.

On the ground

Zebras are born on the open plains. After one hour the foal struggles to its feet and walks with the herd. Its legs are wobbly. It sucks milk for 10 days and then starts to eat grass.

On a rock

This baby **seal** is born on the open rock. After a rest, mother and baby will swim together in the open sea.

How many babies?

An **elephant** has one baby.

An **ostrich** lays
up to 15 eggs.

The **armadillo** has four babies.
They are identical quads.

A **tiger** can have one, two, three or four cubs.

A **Nile crocodile** can lay up to 95 eggs.

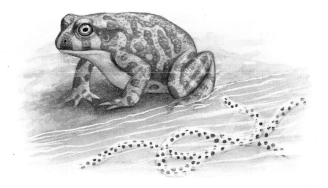

This **toad** lays up to 20,000 eggs.

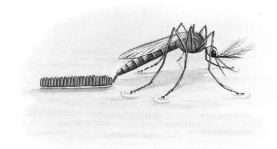

A **mosquito** lays up to 300 eggs.

A **cod** lays 5 million eggs.

Family life

Some babies are looked after by their mother and father.

These baby **swans**, called cygnets *(signets)*, are protected from their enemies. If the cygnets are in danger, the swans will fight with their wings and beaks.

Coyote pups live in a den built by their parents. When they are newly born, the father hunts for the whole family.

Other animals live in larger groups where families live together.

When she has a baby, the mother **elephant** is helped by other females. They all help to protect the elephant calf.

Two **badger** families live in this underground home. It is called a set. The parents make a little room for the cubs. Soon all the badgers will play together.

Caring mothers

Most baby animals are cared for by their mothers.

The mother **crocodile** guards her eggs until they hatch. When they are born, she takes them to a quiet pool in her mouth.

Baby **scorpions** are carried on their mother's back. She protects them with her poisonous sting.

The baby **orang-utan** is very small and weak when it is born. The mother carries it all the time for the first few months.

Caring fathers

In some families the father works hard to look after the young.

The mother **seahorse** lays her eggs in a pouch on the father's belly. He cares for the eggs. Five weeks later he releases nearly one hundred babies.

The male **Darwin frog** keeps the eggs safe in his mouth. They stay there until they are tiny frogs. Then he opens his mouth and the little frogs jump out.

The male **stickleback** builds a nest of weeds. The female lays her eggs inside and swims away. The father then guards the nest and he will look after the babies when they hatch.

Strange families

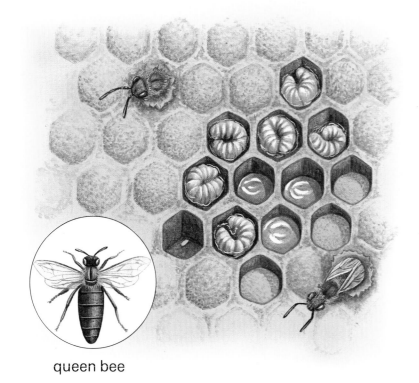

queen bee

These young **bees** all have the same mother. She is the queen bee. Her only job is to lay eggs.

Cuckoos lay their eggs in other birds' nests. The new foster parents will feed and look after the baby cuckoo as if it was their own.

The **spiny anteater** lays one egg. She grows a pouch to keep the egg warm. When the baby grows, it sucks milk from inside the pouch. The pouch will close when the baby no longer needs it.

When they are born these **greenfly** have tiny little eggs inside them. In eight to ten days each greenfly has its own babies. The mother can give birth to 25 babies every day.

Playing and learning

Baby animals learn by playing with each other and watching the older animals.

Chimpanzees play chase in the trees. The babies run and dodge. They learn how to escape from their enemies.

Otters need to catch fish for food. Baby otters must learn to swim fast. They like playing games, making slides and splashing each other.

Bear cubs roll over each other and pretend to fight. This makes them strong. They see the adult bears having real fights.

Some parents teach the young animals how to hunt and find food.

The mother **leopard** teaches her cubs to hunt in the forest. It learns to move quietly and to lie in wait ready to pounce on a passing animal.

The **fox** teaches its cubs to hunt. Cubs must learn to run fast and pounce at the right moment. This adult has some food in his mouth. He holds it just out of reach and runs away. The cubs try to take the food.

Young **beavers** watch their parents find food. They learn which plants are good to eat.

Growing and changing

Some babies do not look like their parents.

Frog

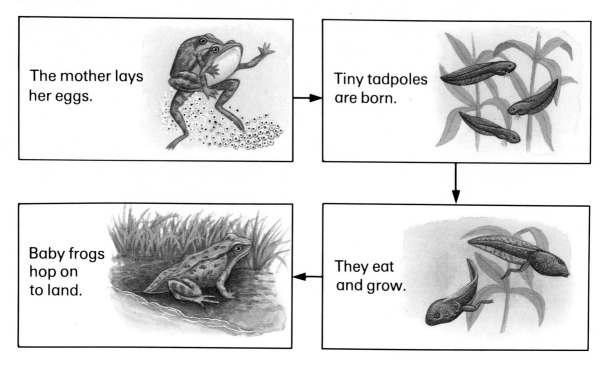

The mother lays her eggs.

Tiny tadpoles are born.

Baby frogs hop on to land.

They eat and grow.

Butterfly

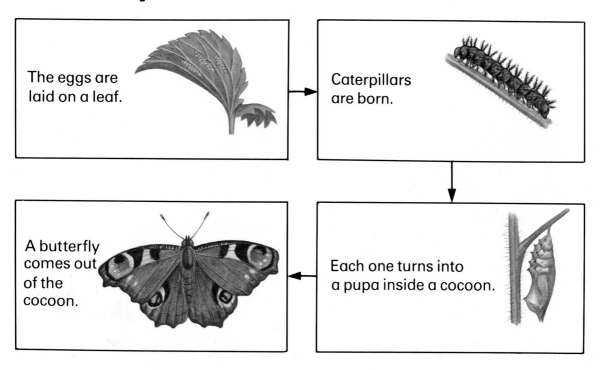

The eggs are laid on a leaf.

Caterpillars are born.

A butterfly comes out of the cocoon.

Each one turns into a pupa inside a cocoon.

These babies look like their parents.

Cricket

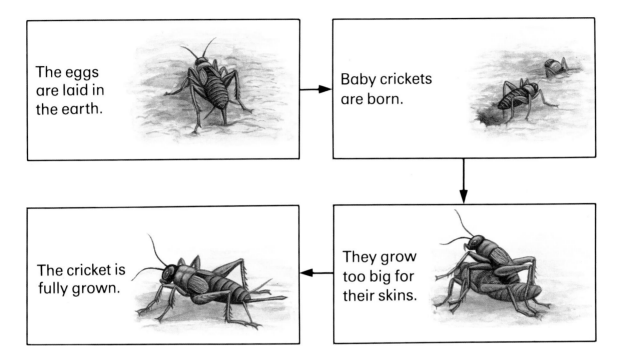

The eggs are laid in the earth.

Baby crickets are born.

The cricket is fully grown.

They grow too big for their skins.

Lion

female

The female cub looks like her mother. The male cub will have a long mane when he grows up.

male

Growing up

Some babies grow up quickly, others grow slowly. It is a long time before they become adult and can have babies of their own.

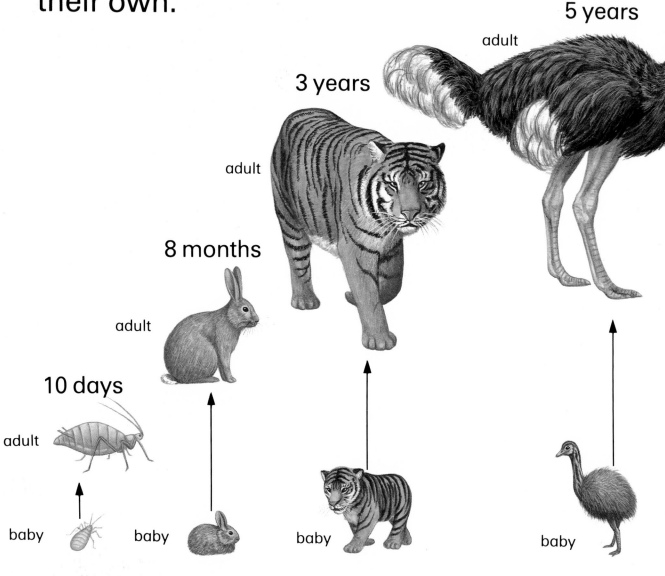

5 years
adult

3 years

adult

8 months

adult

10 days

adult

baby

baby

baby

baby

greenfly   rabbit   tiger   ostrich

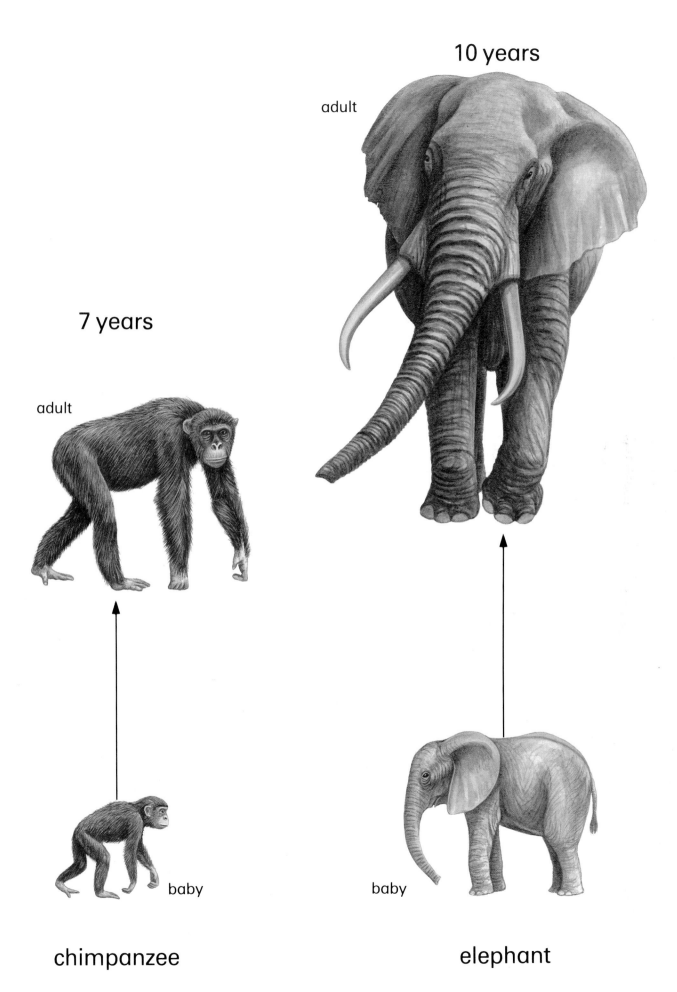

10 years

adult

7 years

adult

baby

baby

chimpanzee

elephant

41

Living Together

Animals together

Animals that live together can help and protect each other.

Canada geese

baboons

polar bears

rattlesnakes

When more than two animals stay together, this is called a group. Some spend their lives in this way, while others form groups at special times of the year.

Living in groups

Animals live together in large or small groups. These groups all have different names.

Chimpanzee groups are called clans. They live in the trees and on the ground. Males sometimes move to live with other clans.

Mandrills live in a group called a troop. The males have bright red and blue faces. They live together in the forest.

Beavers live in a small group called a family – mother, father and babies. The young that were born the year before may also still live with them.

Groups of **kangaroos** are called mobs. Several mobs may join together when they are resting in the shade.

Female **seals** form special groups called harems. One male seal lives with a harem of many female seals.

Soon after these baby seals are born their mothers go back to the sea. The pups live in a group called a pod. The mothers return to the pups to feed them.

These **snapper fish** swim together in groups called schools. They swim close together in the open sea.

Sea birds gather together in groups called colonies. These **gannets** nest together high up in the safety of the cliffs.

Several hundred thousand **flamingoes** also form a huge colony. On the shores of a lake they build nests for their young.

Many bird groups are called flocks. There may be a million birds in a flock of wild **budgerigars**.

Many animals that live in the grasslands of Africa form very large groups called herds.

The **hippopotamus** likes to wallow in mud. At night, the herd leaves the river to look for food on the river bank.

Ostriches are always on the move. They live in large herds. They split into family groups during the rainy season.

Buffalo like to cover themselves with mud. This keeps them cool. It also keeps biting insects away. When the herd moves, young males gather in a special bachelor herd that follows behind the others.

Some **antelopes** form special nursery herds. These are groups of mothers and babies. The males go off to live by themselves.

Leaving the group

The males in some family groups leave to live alone, while the females stay with their young. The male tiger and polar bear both leave their families.

Animals that hunt in teams are usually able to catch their prey, but the lone **tiger** has a harder time to find food.

The male **polar bear** rules the pack ice because it has no enemies. It is a fierce hunter and does not need the safety of a group.

Safety in numbers

By staying together in a group, animals can help and protect each other in many ways.

When **giraffes** are feeding, each animal in the group faces in a different direction. In this way, they can look all around for an approaching lion.

When they are drinking, giraffes spread out their front legs and bend down to the water. In this position they cannot see behind them. The giraffes take turns to drink while others watch out for danger.

Penguin groups are called rookeries. These **Emperor penguins** help each other in the cold. The group huddles together with the chicks in the middle. Each adult rests its beak on the body of the bird in front. Packed tightly together, only a small part of their bodies faces the freezing winds, so they can keep warm.

Musk oxen are often attacked by **wolves** hunting in packs. They cannot outrun the wolves and there is nowhere to hide. The oxen form a circle around the babies. Facing outwards they use their huge curved horns to protect them. The wolves may be speared by the horns, or thrown backwards among the herd and trampled to death.

If **starlings** fly close together they can escape from an enemy. A **falcon** will not attack a flock of birds as it might crash into the flock and hurt itself.

When travelling in search of food, a **baboon** troop stays close together. The mothers and babies walk in the middle surrounded by the strong males. The troop can often scare away an enemy. Under attack, the baboons bare their teeth, make loud screeching noises, and bang and stamp on the ground. This can frighten even a fierce **leopard**.

Signs and signals

Groups of animals need to be able to 'talk' to each other. To do this, they use signs, signals, noises and smells.

Every year **snow geese** set off on long journeys to new feeding grounds. They call out to each other, making loud honking noises when they are ready to leave. They also call out as they fly, to keep the flock together.

These **gazelles** use a signal. If one of the gazelles sees a **cheetah** it flares out the white hairs under its tail. Animals on the edge of the herd see this and move closer. They signal to each other and, sensing the danger, they all run to escape.

Howler monkeys live in the thick forest. Because they cannot always see through the leaves, they call out to each other. They make many different kinds of noises by howling, grunting, groaning and gurgling. If one of them finds a good tree in which to sleep, it calls out to tell the others.

Dolphins swim together in schools. They talk to each other by making chattering and whistling sounds. If a baby dolphin swims too far away, its mother calls it back to the safety of the group.

Each **badger** group lives in a special place in the forest. This is its territory. Badgers mark out their territory using a special gland in their bodies, because they do not want other groups living too near them. The smell tells other badgers that a group is already living there.

Gorillas live in small peaceful groups. They have many ways of telling other groups to keep away from their territory. If two huge males meet, they give each other fierce looks, meaning 'go away'. If this does not work, they roar and bang their chests. The gorillas do not want to fight, so they try to scare off any strangers that come too close to them.

Hunting for food

By living and working together animals have a better chance of hunting and finding the food they need. This can also be shared by the group.

Pelicans help each other to catch fish. A group forms a horseshoe shape. As the pelicans move forwards, they beat their wings on the water. They drive the fish to shallow water where the pelicans catch them.

Killer whales hunt in packs of six or seven. They attack huge right whales. They chase the whale until it is tired out and then share the meal.

Cattle egrets work together. Some of the birds beat the grass with their wings. Others behind them catch the insects that have been disturbed. The egrets then change places.

Jackals live in family groups, but many families join together in packs to hunt large animals. While some of the jackals hunt, others stay behind to look after the cubs. The food is brought back and shared by all the jackals.

Lionesses do most of the hunting for their group, called a pride. They hunt as a team. They catch more food for the pride because they work together.

Caring for each other

Some animals in large groups take great care of each other. They look after the young, the old, the sick and the injured.

Monkeys search each other's fur for dirt and fleas. This is called grooming. Although they do not always have fleas, monkeys enjoy being groomed. It shows friendship and care for one another.

Whales travel in large groups called schools. If one of them is sick or hurt, the whales will not leave it. They try to help the sick animal even if it is dangerous to do so.

Zebras live in family groups which all belong to a large herd. The family is made up of a male with up to ten females and their young. All the animals in the herd care for each other. If one zebra strays away from the herd, the others search for it until it is found.

All the females in an **elephant** herd share in caring for the young. The males watch over the whole herd. If an animal is injured while the herd is on the move, the males support it between them and help it along.

Thousands together

Some insects live together in very large groups. They help each other with the work that needs to be done.

Ants

Some **ants** build nests on the ground made of earth and dead leaves. Thousands of ants live in the colony.

These ants help each other to carry a leaf back to the nest. It will be used to repair a hole.

Ants know each other by smell. If a strange ant comes to the nest, workers drive it away.

Amazon ants attack the nests of **black ants** in armies. They steal the young which they use as slaves. The slaves have to build the nest and feed all the Amazon ants.

Termites

The queen **termite** grows into a long sausage shape. She is full of eggs and cannot move about. Workers swarm over her, carrying away her eggs.

Soldier termites are larger than the others. They guard the nest. They attack enemies and wrap them up with sticky threads.

Wasps

Some **wasps** build a nest with paper. They scrape wood from trees and chew it into a pulp using their powerful jaws. Inside the nest there are many rooms called cells. The queen wasp lays eggs in these cells.

Bees

Inside their nest in a hollow tree worker **honey bees** share all the work. They change jobs as they grow older.

cleaning cells

nursing young

finding food

guarding the nest

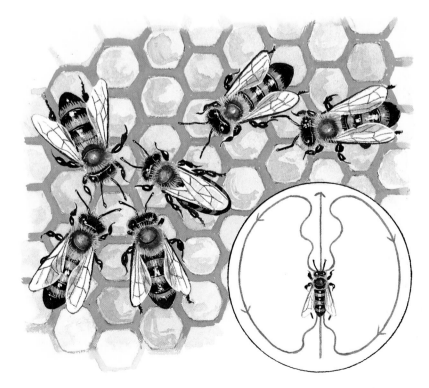

When worker honey bees find some new flowers they return to the nest and dance. As they twist and turn the dance shows the others how far away the flowers are and in which direction the bees must go.

On the move – for food

Animals make long journeys by land, sea and air. This is called migration. These animals migrate in search of food.

Twice a year in North America, **caribou** travel hundreds of miles. In winter, snow and ice cover their feeding grounds. The herd moves south to find food. They feed there until the spring when mosquitoes begin to hatch. To avoid being bitten, the caribou travel back to the north.

These **wolves** hunt the caribou. When the herd moves, the wolves follow behind. Any caribou that cannot keep up with the herd is overtaken and killed for food.

In Africa there is a wet and a dry season every year. **Wildebeest** live on grass, feeding in small groups during the wet season. In the dry season when there is not enough food, groups of wildebeest gather together in enormous herds. They set off on long journeys in search of better grazing.

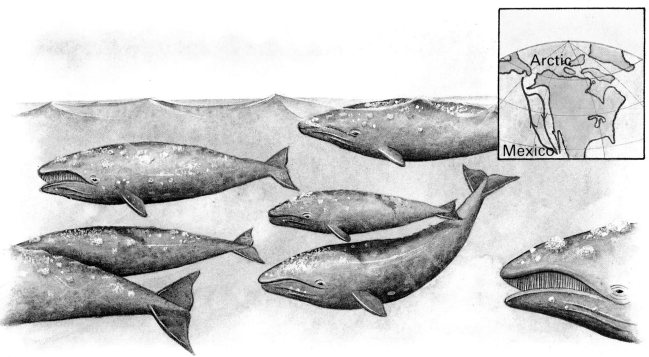

In the summer, **grey whales** feed in the Arctic Ocean. They feed on krill (small shrimps) and they grow very fat. In winter, the sea gets colder so the krill swim down to the sea-bed to escape the cold. Whales cannot feed in such deep waters. They must swim thousands of miles to find food in the warmer seas around Mexico.

Some animals migrate because of overcrowding.

When the weather is good and there is plenty of food, **locusts** have so many babies that there may be too many of them in one place. A swarm of thousands of babies moves off in search of food. The swarm flies down and strips off the leaves from any growing plant they see.

In winter, **lemmings** shelter underground. They tunnel under the snow eating the roots and stems of plants. The plants cannot grow so there will not be enough food for them all in summer. Thousands of them migrate to new places crossing rivers and streams as they go.

On the move – to breed

Some animals gather in groups and migrate many thousands of miles to find the best place to have a family. When animals have young, it is called breeding.

Baby **salmon** are born in freshwater streams. When they are old enough, they swim many miles to the sea. Here they feed and grow. A few years later, the adult salmon make the long journey back up the rivers to the same stream in which they were born. Here they lay their eggs.

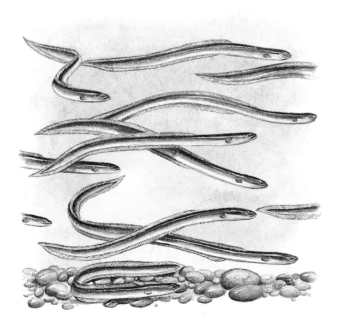

Eels live in rivers, but they swim thousands of miles to breed in the sea. The eels lay their eggs in seaweed. The babies, called elvers, take three years to swim back to the rivers where their parents lived.

Monarch butterflies live alone in summer. When winter comes, thousands of butterflies gather in huge crowds. They fly south to breed in the warm weather. On their journey they rest in trees at night, using the same trees every year.

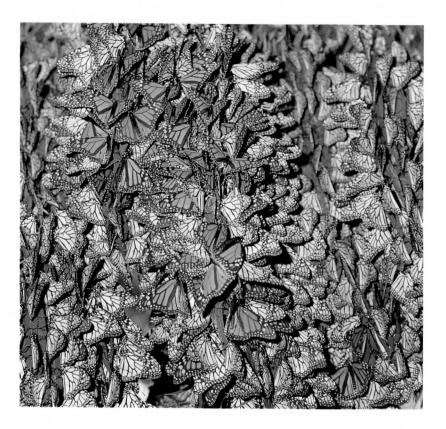

North Pole

South Pole

The **Arctic tern** spends the winter at the South Pole. When spring comes, it flies to the other side of the world. The tern nests and has its young at the North Pole where there is plenty of food for its chicks.

Spiny lobsters live in shallow water. They migrate to deep waters to lay their eggs. When they travel, the lobsters stay together. They follow each other in a long line.

Green turtles travel thousands of miles across oceans to lay their eggs. The turtles gather in large colonies near the shores of small islands. The females leave the sea to lay their eggs on the beach. Then they return to the sea and swim back to their feeding grounds.

Sleeping in winter

Winter is a difficult time for many animals. Some of them hide away and sleep through this cold time. This is called hibernation.

Ladybirds or **ladybugs** escape from the cold by gathering in trees or cracks in rocks. They sleep close together for warmth.

Horseshoe bats feed at night catching insects. In winter there are not many insects to catch, so the bats sleep. They hang upside down from a cave roof holding on with their claws.

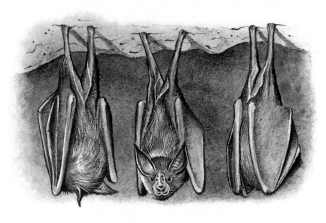

When winter comes, **rattlesnakes** hibernate in large groups. The snakes follow each other's trails to holes or burrows that they use every year. They huddle together, curling round one another.

Keeping warm

It is important for animals to keep warm. Some of them do this by staying very close to each other at different times.

Many birds like these **rooks** gather together in the treetops at night. This is called roosting.

These **bearded reedlings** shelter from the wind in reed beds. They spend the cold nights huddled together for warmth.

These **walruses** live in the cold north. They sleep on top of each other on the beach. There may be thousands of them on one beach.

Living together

Sometimes different kinds of animals live together.

Black garden ants live with **aphids**. The aphids make a sweet liquid that the ants like to eat. The ants take great care of the aphids. They give them shelter in bad weather, look after their eggs and protect them from enemies.

remora

Remoras are tiny fish that live with **sharks**. They fix on to the shark's body using a special sucker. They feed on tiny animals that live on the shark's skin. They also eat scraps of the shark's food when it is feeding.

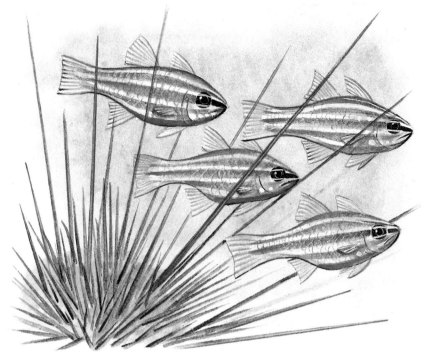

Cardinal fish and **sea urchins** live together in the warm Indian Ocean. In the daytime the fish shelter in the sea urchin's long, sharp spines. They eat small scraps of food that are stuck in the spines.

A **hermit crab** often has two other animals living with it. A tiny **bristle worm** hides inside the crab's shell and a **sea anemone** rides on top of the shell. The anemone's stinging tentacles protect all the animals. The crab is a messy feeder and the others feed on scraps of its food.

Animals must find food and protect themselves to stay alive. Some can do this living alone but many others can only survive by living together.

Nature's Builders

Animal builders

Animals make their homes in every kind of place, hot or cold, wet or dry.

wasp

tailor bird

harvest mouse

badger

beaver

Animals use different parts of their bodies as tools.
Their sharp beaks, strong legs, teeth and claws can build, weave and dig.
Their homes are made of all kinds of materials. They may use grass, leaves, twigs, mud, wood, shells or stones.

Making homes

In and under a tree

Many animals make their homes in trees. The homes are not always the same. Animals may use the leaves, the branches, the trunk or even the roots of a tree.

sugar glider

penduline tit

orang-utan

heron

red squirrel

raccoon

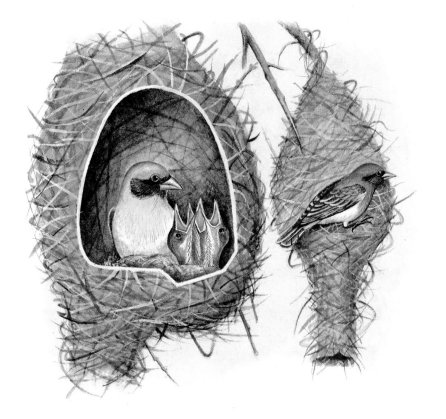

Red-headed weaver birds have two homes. The male builds a strong nest for the female to lay her eggs in. He makes another nest for himself close by. The family use these nests for many years.

A **badger's** underground home is called a set. The entrance is often under the roots of a large tree. Using their sharp claws and powerful front legs, badgers dig tunnels sloping downwards. The tunnels end in large chambers. Some are used for storing food, others for living and sleeping in.

Under the ground

Some other animals make their homes underground. Here they are protected from bad weather. They are also safely hidden from enemies. Many of these animals are powerful diggers.

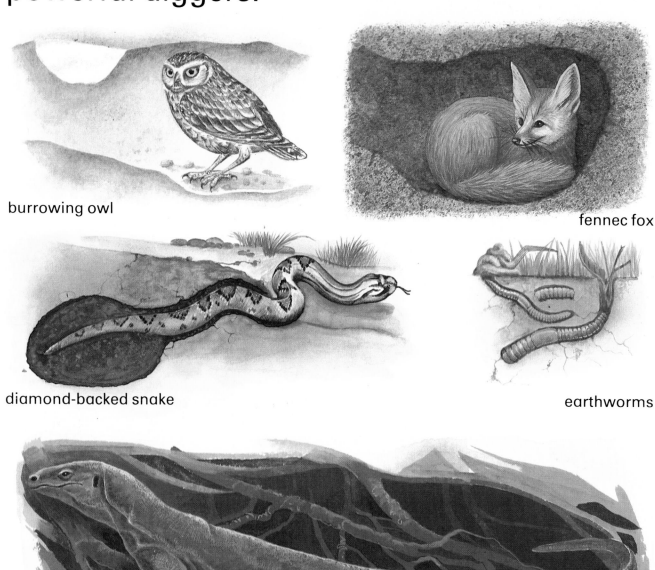

burrowing owl

fennec fox

diamond-backed snake

earthworms

komodo dragon

Rabbits dig burrows, tunnels and escape holes. Their home is called a warren. Female· rabbits line special nursery burrows with their own fur.

A **mole's** home is a hollowed-out nest underground. It is lined with leaves and grass. From the nest, the mole digs many tunnels. Using its sharp claws and strong front legs, it loosens the earth. The mole then turns itself in the tunnel and pushes the loose earth up and out to the surface. This makes a small hill above the ground.

The **chuckwalla** lives in the desert. At night, it digs a hole in the sand to sleep in, protected from cold desert nights.

Many **snakes** living in the desert escape the heat of the day by pushing themselves into the sand.

Jerboas also make a burrow deep under the desert sand where it is cool. The jerboa digs two tunnels leading to the surface. As it enters one tunnel, the end is blocked up with sand. If a **snake** follows it, the jerboa can escape, using the second tunnel.

Near water

Animals that live near rivers dig out their homes in the riverbank.

An **otter's** home is called a holt. Otters dig out a holt in the bank of a river or under the roots of a tree. The entrance tunnel is under the water. It slopes upwards, ending in a large, dry chamber lined with moss and grass.

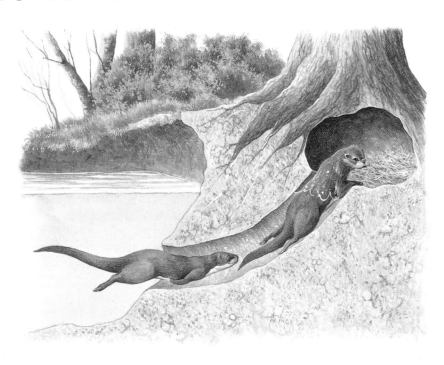

The **kingfisher** uses its sharp, pointed beak to make a tunnel in the riverbank. It lines the nesting chamber with fish bones.

A **pond tortoise** digs into the soft mud at the edge of a pond to make a home for the winter.

Under water

Some animals build homes in water. They are special builders.

The **water spider** spins a bell-shaped web around water plants. It collects air bubbles on its hairy body and carries them underwater. It squeezes the air into the web with its back legs, making many journeys to do this. It eats and sleeps in this underwater home.

Beavers use their sharp teeth to chop down trees. They stick branches and stones together with mud to make a dam across a river. Behind the dam the beavers build a lodge. The nest is above water. Food is stored underwater. The entrances are underwater so the beavers can reach their food even when the water is frozen over.

In high places

Nests in cliffs or on rocky ledges make very safe homes.

These **bee-eaters** make their homes in sandy cliffs. They dig out a nesting hole with their strong beaks. Many bee-eaters live close together.

Golden eagles build nests for their young on rocky ledges high up in the mountains. They weave a nest of twigs which they return to every year.

Puffins spend most of their time in the sea, but they make a home for their young in the cliffs. Using their beaks and feet they make a long tunnel. At the end of this tunnel they dig out a large nesting chamber.

A home together

Some animals live together in large groups. It is safer and they can help each other to make homes.

Prairie dogs live together in towns underground. They build a raised mound at each entrance hole so that rain water cannot flood their tunnels. They clear away all the grass and plants growing near their homes so that enemies cannot creep up on them. Guards watch out for any danger.

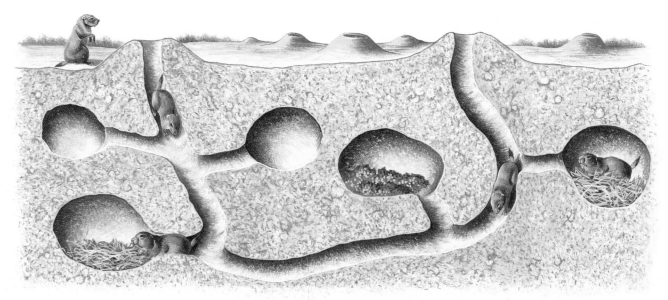

Deep underground, each animal has its own nesting chamber. These are joined by tunnels leading to storerooms where food is kept for the winter.

Social weaver birds join together to build a huge home. They weave grasses to make a roof. Under this roof each pair of birds builds a bottle-shaped nest. Every year, new nests are built under the old ones.

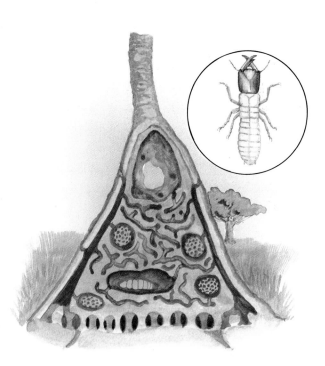

Millions of **termites** live together in huge towers which they build out of earth and mud. The mud is baked by the hot sun and becomes rock hard.

Inside the mound there are living rooms, storerooms and nurseries for the young. All the termites have the same mother and father, who live together in the largest chamber in the middle of the nest. Blind workers build the nest and collect food. Soldier termites guard the nest.

Sharing a home

Sometimes different animals live together, sharing the same home.

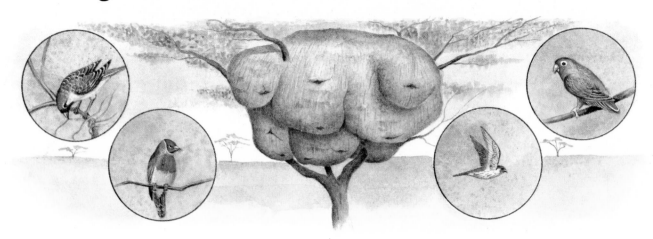

At times, the **social weaver birds** are joined by other birds. **Red-headed finches, pygmy falcons** and **lovebirds** make their homes in empty nests.

The **osprey** or **fish hawk** builds a large nest with sticks and branches at the top of a dead tree. Smaller birds like **wrens** or **sparrows** build their homes in the side of this nest. Although the osprey is a bird of prey it eats only fish, so all the birds live happily together.

This bird called a **sooty shearwater** shares its burrow with a **tuatara**. The tuatara is very slow moving and too lazy to make its own home. It does not harm the bird. They can share a home because the bird searches for food in the daytime and the tuatara hunts at night.

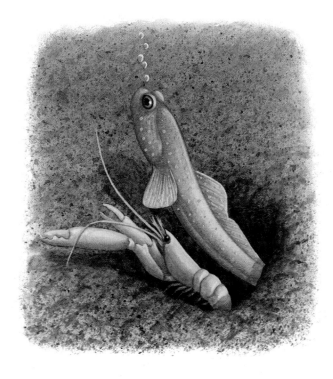

This **pistal prawn** digs a burrow in the sand and shares it with a **goby fish**. The goby sits in the entrance to the hole keeping watch. If an enemy approaches, the fish disappears inside the burrow warning the prawn to hide as well.

Any hole is home

Some animals do not build their own homes. They use any hole or burrow they can find.

The hole in this cactus was made by a **woodpecker**. When the woodpecker left its nest the **elf owls** moved in.

The **burrowing owl** makes its nest in the burrow of another animal. Sometimes it will share with the animal. This owl lives with **prairie dogs**. It spends most of its time outside the burrow looking for food.

This **blenny fish** lives anywhere it can find shelter – a crack in the rock, under stones, even in a broken bottle.

The **striped hyena** lives in caves or old buildings. Animal bones at the entrance show where the hyena's den is.

The **spotted hyena** makes its home in an empty anteater's nest.

This **red fox** has found an empty hole. Inside it has made tunnels and chambers. Its home is called an earth. The fox spends most of the daytime inside, going out at night to hunt.

Carrying a home

These animals do not need to build a home. They carry it with them.

The **garden snail** has a shell which is part of its body. Wherever the snail goes, its shell gives it shelter and protection.

The **tortoise** also has a shell. It grows bigger as the tortoise grows. When in danger, the tortoise pulls its head and legs up into the shell. The hard shell protects its soft body.

This female **wallaby** does not carry her own home but carries a special home for her baby. The baby lives in a pouch on the mother's stomach for many months.

This **turtle** lives in rivers. The turtle can rest on the river bottom and stretch its long neck up out of the water to breathe. If an enemy comes near, it pulls back into its shell.

Moving house

As some animals move from place to place they must build or find new homes to live in.

Killer bees fly in swarms searching for food. Wherever they land, the bees find a new home. This may be an empty box, a tin can, a crack in a building, or an empty burrow.

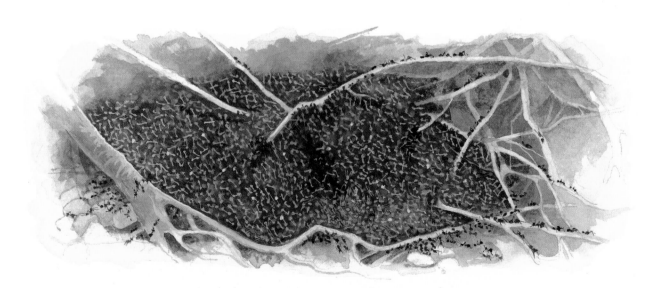

These **army ants** also carry out swarm raids, sometimes staying up to three weeks in one place. Here they make homes in hollow trees or under rocks. Thousands of ants hook onto each other to make a kind of tent. The queen ant and her eggs are safe inside.

Chimpanzees move around in the forest searching for food. Every night they sleep in a new place. They build a nest high in the trees. Each animal builds a platform made of broken branches and then bends twigs over it for a roof. The chimpanzee uses leafy branches to make a soft bed on this platform.

The **hermit crab** does not grow its own shell. It lives in empty whelk shells. When the crab grows too big for one shell it searches for a bigger one. It measures the new shell with its front claws. If it is the right size, the crab climbs in.

A home for the babies

Some animals that do not have a home for most of the year will build a home when they have babies.

Ovenbirds make strong mud nests that are windproof and waterproof. They build from the bottom of the nest upwards in layers ending in a dome shape.

The female **king cobra** makes a nest hidden in the forest. She collects leaves to make a soft bed. She coils herself around her eggs to keep them warm.

Hornbills make a safe home for their young in a hole in a tree. The mother bird stays inside the nest with her chicks. Here they are safe from attack by snakes and monkeys. When the chicks are ready to fly she breaks open the nest to free them all.

Brown bears make a winter den. The bear either digs a den under a rotten tree or finds a cave. It spends the winter asleep and has its cubs in the spring.

The **dormouse** always has a home but makes an extra one for its babies.

During the winter the dormouse has an underground home. It sleeps rolled in a ball wrapped in grass. In spring the dormouse makes a new home. It builds a loosely woven nest of grass. When the dormouse has babies, it makes a special nursery nest. This nest is bigger and is lined with soft moss and leaves.

Home is a safe place

Animals must always be on the look out for danger. They may be the next meal for a hungry hunter. These animals build special homes to protect themselves or their babies.

The **mourning dove** makes its nest deep in the spines of a cactus. The sharp spines protect the eggs and the baby birds from enemies.

This **gambels quail** builds its nest under clumps of prickly pear cactus. The sharp spines help to keep lizards away. The male guards the tunnel to this spiky home.

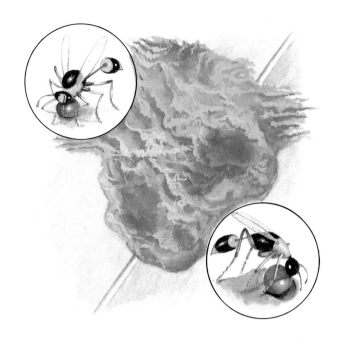

This **mud-dauber wasp** collects soft, wet mud with its front legs and builds a nest for its egg. The wasp seals up the entrance hole by spreading runny mud over it with its jaws. The mud dries hard in the hot sun and the egg is safe inside.

The **caddis fly larva** builds a tube around its soft body made of small stones or shells. Inside this armour it is safe from water spiders. Fish may not see it hidden against stones of the riverbed. As it grows, the larva adds more pieces to its tube.

The **garden eel** digs a tube-like hole in the sea bed. It floats upright held firm in the sand by its tail. If in danger, it disappears quickly into its hole. It never leaves the safety of its home.

Somewhere to sleep

Some animals have a special resting place for sleeping.

Sea otters have no special home. They live in groups close to the shore near beds of seaweed called kelp. When they want to sleep, they wrap themselves up in the long strands of seaweed. This stops them from drifting away from each other.

The **rainbow parrot fish** spins a web around itself when it settles down to sleep.

Snow leopards live high in the mountains. They hunt at night. During the day, the leopard finds a place to rest. This is called its lair. It may be in a cave or under a hollow tree.

Reef sharks are fierce hunters. Sometimes they swim into caves for a rest. In the caves they lie very still but they are not asleep. Their eyes are always open. These sharks become calm and peaceful when they are resting.

Hidden attackers

The **moray eel** ambushes animals from its home. The eel lives in a crack in the rock. When a fish or a lobster swims past, the eel darts out and catches it.

The **octopus** lives on the sea bed which is covered in rocks and stones. Often an octopus will move stones around itself to make a lair. It hides in the lair, darting out to catch food.

The **trapdoor spider** digs a burrow covered by a lid. In the daytime, the spider hides in its burrow. At night it opens the lid a little and watches. When the spider sees its prey, it springs open the lid and dashes out.

Scorpions live in rocky cracks or burrows in the sand. They dig deep into the sand with their front legs to hide from the hot desert sun. At night, they come out to hunt.

Unusual homes

These are some of the strange homes animals have.

1

2

3

4

This **leaf-rolling weevil** makes a home for its egg. It uses a leaf that is still growing on the branch of a tree. It rolls and twists the leaf, wrapping its egg safely inside.

This little **pearl fish** has a home inside the body of another animal. The **sea cucumber** is a long tube-like animal. At night, the pearl fish swims about searching for food. It then wriggles back inside the sea cucumber and hides.

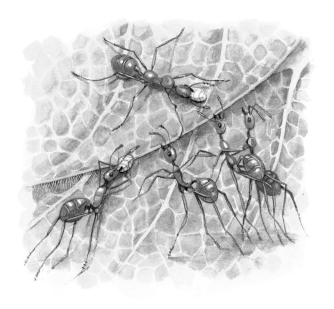

Weaver ants use their young grubs to help them make a nest. The grubs make silk in their mouths. As some of the ants pull leaves together, others holding the grubs, criss-cross from side to side. The silk sticks the leaves together making a waterproof home.

These **ants** bite tiny holes in the thick thorns of a tree and make their nest inside.

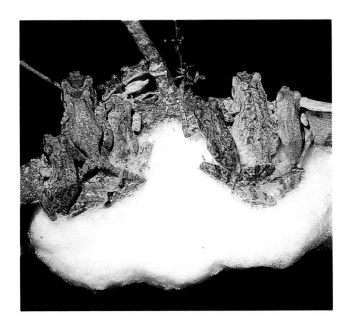

These **frogs** make their nest by beating egg jelly from inside their bodies into a foam using their back legs. The nest is on a branch over the water. The outside of this foam nest hardens to protect the eggs inside. Later, the nest softens. Tadpoles wriggle out and drop into the water below.

Nature's builders

These animals are expert builders. Each one uses its body in a different way.

The **leaf-curling spider** makes a leaf shelter next to its web. Using a silk thread the spider spins silk across the leaf. As the silk dries it shrinks. This curls the leaf into a tube shape. This spider could be called one of the engineers of the animal world.

The **sandmason worm** makes an underwater burrow in the sand. Above its hole it builds a 'tree' of sand to trap its food. It picks up sand grains one at a time with its tentacles and sticks them together making the tree shape.

Many other animals are clever builders.

The **tailor bird** makes its nest by sewing together two leaves. The bird makes holes along the edges of the leaves with its sharp beak. It threads grass through the holes to join the nest together. Inside, a soft bed is made with grass.

The **harvest mouse** builds a home from wheat grass. It balances on a stalk, holding on with its back legs and tail. It then weaves strips of wheat grass round the plant stalk to make a nest.

Homes of all shapes and sizes give animals warmth, shelter and protection. They are places in which to eat, sleep and raise a family.

Staying Alive

Finding food

Animals have many different ways of finding their food.

Plant eaters must learn where to find the best food and how to avoid their enemies. Meat eaters need to learn how to catch and kill for their food. Animals that catch and eat other animals are called predators. The animal that they catch is called their prey. Animals do their best to escape being captured by these hunters.

Meat eaters

Animals that hunt and kill other animals to eat are called carnivores. Most of them have very good eyesight and hearing. Many of them can move fast. Some have sharp claws and teeth.

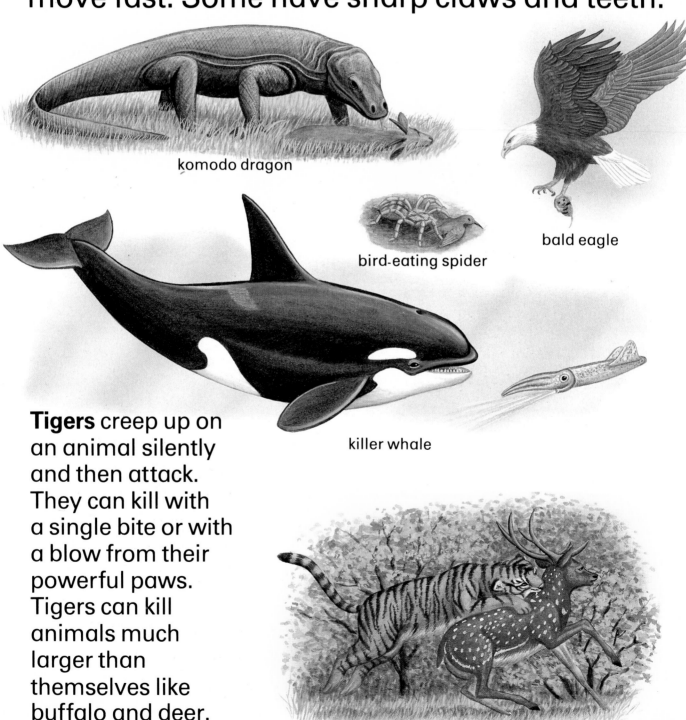

komodo dragon

bird-eating spider

bald eagle

killer whale

Tigers creep up on an animal silently and then attack. They can kill with a single bite or with a blow from their powerful paws. Tigers can kill animals much larger than themselves like buffalo and deer.

Fish eaters

These animals are carnivores but they eat fish.

heron

shark

otter

crocodile

Most bears move so slowly that they cannot catch their prey in a chase. The **grizzly bear** waits by the side of a river. As salmon swim along, the grizzly bear flips them out of the water with its powerful paws.

Plant eaters

Some animals never eat meat. They eat plants, fruit, grasses and leaves. They are called herbivores. They have strong teeth to bite off and grind their food. As they can only take small mouthfuls, they spend a lot of time eating.

reindeer

orang-utan

koala

zebra

The **black rhinoceros** eats leaves and twigs. It has a special top lip which folds into a small point. The rhino uses its lip to pick leaves from trees and bushes.

Eating all sorts

Animals that eat meat and plants are called omnivores. They have a wider choice of food than other animals. As the seasons change they eat whatever food they can find.

sea turtle

jackal

thrush

badger

The **raccoon** eats frogs, birds, insects, eggs, fruit and berries. It searches underneath stones in rivers and streams, using its long thin fingers to find food.

Gentle giants

These giants of the animal world are not the deadly killers we might think. Some eat plants and others eat very tiny sea creatures.

Gorillas are gentle vegetarians. They do not harm any other animals to get their food. They feed on leaves, ferns, roots and shoots. Their food is so juicy that they never need to drink.

Elephants are plant eaters. They feed on leaves and grass. They can tear up whole trees and eat the leaves, branches and thorns. Their huge teeth are worn down by this rough food. In its lifetime an elephant will use up six sets of teeth.

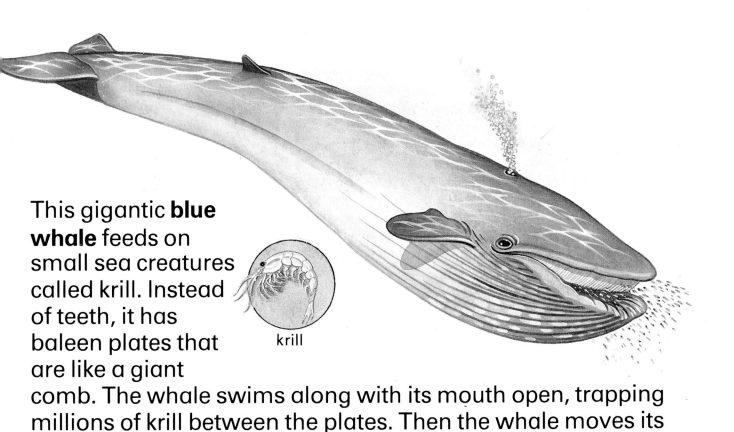

This gigantic **blue whale** feeds on small sea creatures called krill. Instead of teeth, it has baleen plates that are like a giant comb. The whale swims along with its mouth open, trapping millions of krill between the plates. Then the whale moves its tongue to push out the water and swallows the krill.

krill

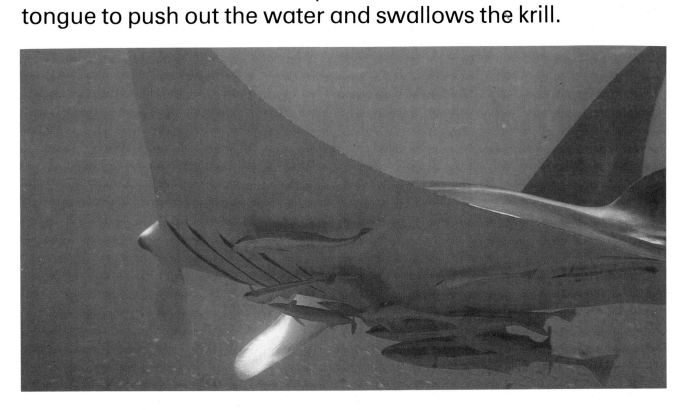

Most sea creatures are also safe from the **giant manta ray.** Although it looks fierce, it hardly ever attacks anything larger than a small fish. It feeds mainly on krill which it scoops up from the sea using horns at the side of its mouth.

Hunters

Most meat eaters hunt for their food. Some creep up on their prey. This is called stalking. They learn to move quietly and attack suddenly.

The **cheetah** stalks silently towards the feeding herd of gazelles. With no enemy to be seen, the gazelles continue feeding.
The cheetah watches the herd, deciding which animal to attack. When it is near enough, the cheetah will burst into the chase with lightning speed.

fangs

The **rattlesnake** slides silently through the undergrowth, stalking its prey. It smells with its tongue. Small pits between its eyes can feel the warmth of any animal hidden in the darkness of the night. Suddenly the rattlesnake strikes out and bites its victim with poisonous fangs.

Other hunters lie in wait for their prey.
These animals must learn to wait patiently
and quietly before they attack.

The **polar bear** is sitting silently by a hole in the ice, waiting for
a seal to appear. When the seal comes up to breathe, the polar
bear will pull it quickly out of the water, kill it and eat it.

Many insects do not notice
the **praying mantis** until it is
too late. This hunter sits
patiently in the bushes
nodding its head, just like the
flowers moving in the wind.
It waits for an insect to come
close, then attacks suddenly
with its spiky front legs.

Trappers

Many animals cannot move quickly or they are small and weak. They have special tricks to help them catch their food.

This turtle, the **alligator snapper,** lies still on the river bed with its mouth open. Two pink growths hanging from its tongue look just like juicy worms to any fish swimming nearby. This is a clever trap. As a fish swims up for a meal it is eaten by the turtle.

The **decoy fish** uses a clever trick to catch its prey. Its fin looks like a little fish with an eye and an open mouth. When hungry fish swim up to have a closer look, the decoy fish swallows them.

Some animals make their own traps.

The ant lion larva feeds on ants. It digs a deep hole to catch them.

1
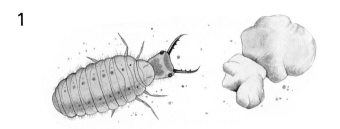

The ant lion begins to dig in the sand.

2

With its strong jaws it clears away small stones.

3

Larger stones are pushed up and out of the hole.

4

The ant lion digs deeper until the sides are very steep.

5

6

It hides under the sand at the bottom of its trap.
As soon as an ant touches the edge, the sand on the slope
slides downwards taking the ant with it. As it struggles
the ant slides faster to the bottom where it is caught.

Using tools

These animals have learned to use materials around them to help them catch or eat their food

Chimpanzees can make tools to catch ants hidden inside a nest. They tear a small branch from a bush and pull off the leaves to make a stick. They then push the stick into the nest and when it comes out it is covered in juicy ants.

The **raft spider** feeds on insects that live in ponds. To get near enough to catch these insects, the spider uses a leaf as a raft. The spider throws the raft onto the water and floats around searching for food.

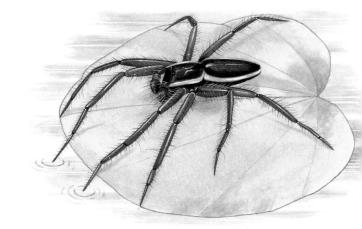

The **sea otter** uses a tool to open very hard shellfish.
It swims down to the sea bed bringing back a flat stone.
Lying on its back with the stone on its belly, the otter hits
the shellfish hard on the stone, breaking the shell open.

This **finch** feeds on grubs that
are hidden in the tree bark.
The bird cannot reach the
grubs with its beak. It uses
a tool to help. The finch
breaks off a long cactus
spine. Holding this in its beak
it digs the spine into cracks
and holes spearing the grubs.

Unusual feeders

These animals all have strange ways of getting their food. Some grow their own food. Some help one another in finding food.

Leaf cutting ants grow their own food. With scissor-like jaws they cut pieces of leaf and carry them back to the nest. The pieces are chewed up into a mushy pulp which is spread out to make a garden. A special fungus grows on this. The ants eat the fungus.

Marine iguanas are pestered by little insects called ticks. As the iguanas lie in the sun, **red rock crabs** crawl all over them eating the ticks. This is an easy way for the crabs to find food.

Whales are pestered by whale lice that dig into their skin and lay eggs. They swim to warmer seas where **phalarope birds** live. As the whales surface, the birds land on their backs to feed on the lice.

When the **great honey guide bird** finds a wild bees' nest, it calls to a **honey badger**. The bird leads the way. Using its sharp claws, the honey badger opens the nest and both feed on the honey.

Avoiding enemies

Hiding

Nature has given some animals special protection. The colour of their bodies helps them to hide from enemies. This is called camouflage.

The **gecko** is camouflaged against the bark of a tree. Because it is so difficult to see, the gecko can rest or sleep, safe from its enemies.

Lying very still this **viper** is nearly invisible on a bed of fallen leaves. Animals looking for food will not notice it.

Some animals can change their body colour to match their surroundings.

The **chameleon** can change colour. On a leaf it will be green.
Against the bark of a tree it can change to red or brown.
Not only is it hidden from enemies, the chameleon can also
wait to attack its own prey without being seen.

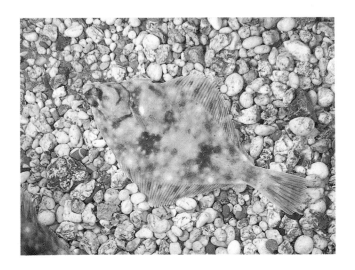

plaice

squid

These sea creatures can also change colour to suit
their backgrounds. When it lies on gravel, the smooth skin
of the **plaice** becomes speckled to match the stones. The **squid**
flashes coloured light patterns which confuse predators.

Other animals have special tricks to hide. They look like something else.

This **leafy sea dragon** could be mistaken for a piece of seaweed. All over its body, flaps of green skin dangle and wave as it floats through the water.

When a **leaf fish** is in danger, it stops swimming, turns on its side and floats. It looks like a dead leaf. It even has a short stump, just like a leaf stalk, on the end of its nose.

Hiding upside down among the spines of a sea urchin, the **shrimp fish** can avoid its enemies. The black lines along its body look like the sea urchin's spines, making it difficult to see.

The **giant peacock moth** has a pattern on its wings. The pattern looks like two large eyes. When the moth lands on a leaf, its wings carry on moving and the false eyes seem to blink. Because they look like the eyes of a large animal, enemies keep away.

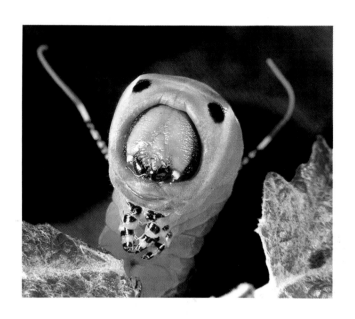

On the end of this **puss moth caterpillar**'s body are special markings that look like a fierce face. If in danger, the caterpillar raises its tail to show the face. This frightens enemies away.

This **hairstreak butterfly**'s markings protect its soft body from enemies. On the back wings it has dots that look like eyes, and false feelers at the bottom of its wings. This looks like a false head. Attacking birds will peck at the false head and the butterfly will escape.

Warning colours

These animals do not need to hide. Their bright colours and markings warn other animals that they are dangerous to eat, and may have a poisonous bite or sting.

ladybird (ladybug)

arrow poison frog

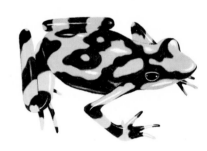

crayfish

ring necked snake

bee

sedge frog

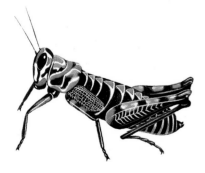

sunset grasshopper

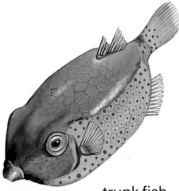

trunk fish

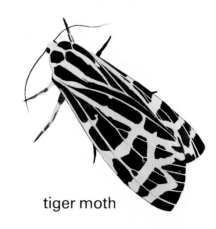

tiger moth

When the **shingle-backed lizard** is attacked, it cannot run away because it is so fat. Instead the lizard opens its mouth wide to show a bright blue tongue. Its enemies know that any bright colour means danger.

Burnet moths have a poison called cyanide inside their bodies. The moth's bright colours warn birds that it is unpleasant to eat.

Copying a warning

These animals are protected by their colouring in a different way. They copy nature's warning colours so that enemies will leave them alone. They are really harmless.

milk snake

coral snake

The **milk snake** is protected from predators because it looks just like a poisonous **coral snake**. The milk snake is not poisonous at all but its enemies cannot tell the difference.

hoverfly

wasp

The dangerous looking **hoverfly** is really quite harmless. It is safe from attack because it looks almost like a **wasp.** Predators think they will be stung if they eat it.

Copying a shape

Other insects are protected by their shape. They each look like part of a plant.

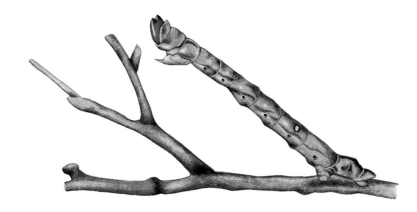

Animals are tricked by the **inchworm**. Standing completely still on a branch, the insect looks like a twig.

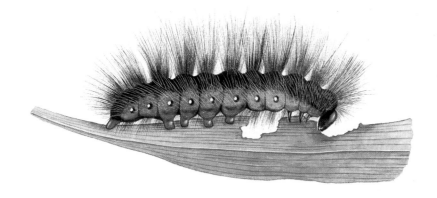

This **cryptic caterpillar** is covered in fine hairs. It could be mistaken for a fluffy seed blowing in the wind.

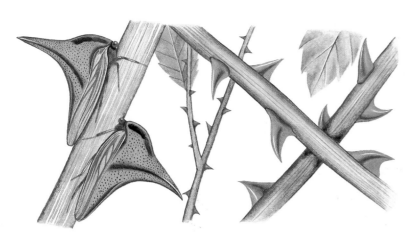

Living together in large groups, **thorn bugs** look just like the other thorns growing on this bush. They will not be noticed until they move.

Warning of danger

Animals are always on the look-out for danger. They have different ways of warning each other.

The **piapiac** (*pie-a-pie-ack*) and the **rhinoceros** have a special partnership. The bird clings on to the rhino's back, feeding on ticks. From this position it can see a long way. This helps the rhino who has very poor eyesight. If the bird sees an enemy it will call out loudly. It will even peck at the rhino's head to warn it of danger.

Prairie dogs have guards outside their burrows. They bark if an enemy appears.

As a warning, **rabbits** stamp on the ground with their back foot.

Elephants have a special way of keeping in touch with each other. They make soft rumbling noises in their throats all the time they are feeding. This noise stops immediately if an enemy is near. Silence means danger.

Bees use smell as a warning. Outside the nest, guard bees keep a look-out for any danger. If an animal comes to the nest, the guards give out a special scent (smell), whirring their wings to spread the smell. Other bees from inside will quickly come to help the guards protect the nest.

Defensive weapons

Many animals cannot escape quickly or hide away from their enemies. They need to defend themselves. Some animals have a weapon.

This **millipede** uses poisonous gas as a weapon. It has a line of little holes along either side of its body. The millipede will fire the gas at an attacker. When it is very scared the millipede shoots from all holes at once leaving behind a cloud of poison.

When it is attacked, the **skunk** squirts out two jets of liquid. This smells so disgusting that most animals run away. The liquid can also blind the skunk's enemies for a short time, giving it a chance of escape.

The **wood ant** squirts dangerous acid at any attacker.

The **black wasp** has a nasty sting which it uses if attacked.

When a **porcupine** is attacked it uses its quills as a weapon. First it shakes its body, rattling the quills as a warning. If the enemy does not run off, the porcupine turns round and charges backwards. It stabs the sharp quills into the animal's face. The quills break off easily leaving the predator full of painful spines.

Escape

Some animals escape from their predators.

If an **octopus** is attacked it squirts a jet of black ink out of a special tube called a siphon. Hidden by clouds of ink the octopus escapes. If it needs to move quickly the octopus can pump water through its siphon. This pushes it quickly along and out of danger.

Pronghorns are excellent runners. They live in the open grassland with nowhere to hide from predators. If they could not escape from enemies, pronghorns would all be killed off. When the herd is attacked by wolves, they run so fast that most of them escape. Only young, weak or sick animals are caught.

If a bird grabs this **lizard** by the tail, the tail breaks off but carries on wriggling. The bird is surprised and the lizard has a chance to escape.

When animals attack the **basilisk lizard** it escapes across the water. It can run so fast across the surface that it does not sink.

Other animals cannot escape by running away from danger. The **manatee** is a huge sea cow. It moves very slowly and cannot defend itself against enemies. It is safe because it lives in places that its enemies cannot reach. The muddy water is too salty for alligators and not deep enough for sharks.

Staying alive

All animals need the food that is in plants.
If there were no plants, there would be no life.
Some animals eat plants, other animals eat
plant eaters. Each has its place in a food chain.

leaf

caterpillar

blue tit

sparrow
hawk

Staying alive is difficult for the plant eaters. These **dikdiks** live
in fear of the hunters and must always keep watch.

Hunters do not attack animals just to harm them. This **fox** must kill to provide food for itself and its family.

Life is not always easy for the hunters. The **cheetah** must eat quickly or move its kill to a safer place. It may be stolen by a pack of **hyenas**. In large numbers the hyenas can overcome even the fiercest cheetah.

The **jaguar** has a better chance of catching a weak animal. The hunter is not always successful. Many animals escape!

In the Wild

Life in the wild

Animals live in wild places all over the world. Each place has different kinds of animal.

lemur

musk ox

crocodile

camel

Animals living in the desert could not live in the cold or in the water. Every animal lives in the best place for it to find food and have its home.

Changes

Animals' bodies change to suit the place where they live. This change is called adaptation. Changes take place over many thousands of years.

The **mudskipper** is a fish that can travel on land. Its body has adapted so that it can come out of the water to look for food. Its bony fins push it across the mud. It can even climb trees.

Peppered moths hide against tree bark. Factory smoke from nearby cities turned trees black. The moths could be seen and many were eaten. They had to change to stay alive.

Some of the moths had black wings. These escaped. Slowly, over 100 years, more black moths survived. Now they can hide in safety.

Penguins live at the cold South Pole where they have no enemies on land. A bird's life is much easier if it can stay on the ground in safety. Over the years, penguins' bodies have changed. They now have webbed feet and flippers instead of wings. These are shaped for fast swimming.

This **tortoise** lives on an island where there is plenty of rain. It feeds on plants near to the ground.

This **tortoise** lives on a dry island. It has a longer neck to reach plants higher up.

The **fennec fox** lives in the hot desert. It has very large ears. As it gets hot, heat is passed out into the air through its ears. This helps to keep the fox cool.

The **red fox** lives in woodlands. It never gets too hot, so it has medium sized ears.

The **arctic fox** lives where it is very cold. Its ears are small so that the warmth of its body is kept inside.

Tree frogs live in jungles. They have sticky pads on their toes so that they can walk and cling on to smooth tree trunks and leaves.

Frogs that live in water have webbed feet. This helps them to swim faster.

Flying frogs also have webbed feet but these are used like a parachute. They leap into the air and gently glide from tree to tree.

As summer changes to winter, many animals change the way they look.

In summer the **ptarmigan** *(tar-mi-gan)* has brownish feathers. In winter its feathers change to white. The bird cannot be seen easily against the white snow. Its feathers become very thick and even cover its feet to keep the bird warm.

This **varying hare** has thin, brown fur. When winter comes its fur changes. It becomes much thicker and turns white. This helps the hare to hide from its enemies.

Living in the trees

Animals that live in the trees are not usually very big. They must be able to climb, jump or swing through the branches.

Chameleons move slowly along the branches holding on tightly with their feet and tails. They have special eyes. One eye can look backwards and the other forwards at the same time.

Lemurs can hold on to the branches with their hands and feet. They are expert at jumping and can move very quickly through the forest. Their eyes face the front which helps them to see how far away the next tree is before they jump.

Living in the water

Many animals live in the water. Some can breathe underwater, but some have to come up to the surface for air.

This **sperm whale's** shape helps it to move easily through the water. It pushes itself along by moving its huge tail up and down. Whales have nostrils called blowholes on top of their heads.

Seals live in very cold seas. They have a thick layer of fat under their skins called blubber. This keeps them warm.

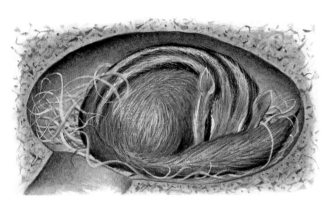

Chipmunks curl up and go to sleep in their warm burrows.

Lemmings live underground. It is warmer under the snow.

The **musk ox** has very thick fur.

The **lynx** has thick fur and big hairy feet to walk on the snow.

Animals in danger

People do not always care about or protect wild animals.

Many have been hunted and killed. Others are in danger of losing their special place to live. Animals can adapt to certain changes but other changes may lead to death.

Some farmers use chemicals to kill insects on their crops. Small birds eat these insects. **Peregrine falcons** that feed on these small birds will also eat the poison and many will die.

Some **otters** live in rivers. As more towns are built nearby, and more people use the rivers for fishing and boating, the otters are scared away. There are not many places for them to go.

The **sea otter** has soft fur that traps air next to its skin. This keeps the otter warm and dry. If a ship spills oil into the sea, the otter's fur cannot protect it and it will die from the cold.

Rain forest animals are also in danger. As forests are cleared to build cities, roads and farms, the animals will have nowhere to live. Animals need wild places to live in. If different kinds of animal die out, they will be lost to us forever. Some countries make laws to protect wild animals. Many have special areas of land called reserves where wild animals can live in safety.

Index

Acknowledgements
ARDEA: 12U (D Burgess); 15B (L & T Bomford); 16U (W Weisser); 18U (B Bevan); 19U (I Beames); 25B (F Gohier); 26BL (A Warren); 31U (J P Ferrero); 33B (W Moller); 74 (P Steyn); 112U (I Beames); 113B (V Taylor); 119U (F Gohier); 122U (H & J Beste); 122B (P Morris) 123UL (P Steyn); 123UR (A Weaving); 128BR (A Lindau); 130BL (F Gohier); 135B (F Gohier); 144CR (E Dragesco); 144CL (E Dragesco); 145U (R Beames). BRUCE COLEMAN: 10 (D & M Plage); 42 (M P Kahl); 44U (H Albrecht); 45B (G Bingham); 46C (Dr E Pott); 47U (R Wilmshurst); 55U (M P Kahl); 66U (F Saver); 69U (R Schroeder); 93U (H Albrecht); 144BL (C Ott); 144BR (C Ott); 145B (N Myers); 148U (N Tomalin); 148B (L Lyon); 151U (R J Tulloch). FRANK LANE: 13U (Silvestris/Frank Lane); 21U (S McCutcheon); 22U (W Wisniewski); 26U (Silvestris/ Frank Lane); 29U (F Hartmann); 50B (C Carvalho); 64U (M Newman); 67U (R Thompson); 71B (W Wisniewski); 84U (M Newman); 85U (W Wisniewski); 85C (A Christiensen); 88U (L W Walker); 91U (R P Lawrence); 127B (A J Roberts); 140U (C Carvalho). NHPA: 15U (A Bannister); 23B (ANT/NHPA); 27U (E H Rao); 28U (E A James); 46U (B Hawkes); 47B (L H Newman); 59U (P Fagot); 65U (A Bannister); 70C (M W F Tweedie); 72U (G I Bernard); 79U (M Leach); 82U (Agence Native); 83UR (J Jeffery); 83UL (P Johnson); 89B (S Dalton); 90U (J & M Bain); 95U (H Teyn); 100B (A Bannister); 100U (B Wood); 115B (A Bannister); 123BL (S Dalton); 141BL (J Kroener); 150B (Orion Press); 152B (S Kracemann); 152U (ANT). NATURAL SCIENCE PHOTOS: 125C (C F E Smedley). OXFORD SCIENTIFIC FILMS: 30B (J A L Cooke); 34B (G I Bernard); 52U (D Allan); 120U (G Merlen); 124U (R H Kuiter) 128UL (Z Leszczynski); 128BL (G A Maclean); 131B (D Thompson). SEAPHOT: 46B (K Amsler); 97B (H Voigtmann); 99B (H Voigtmann). SURVIVAL ANGLIA: 13C (C Buxton/A Price); 22 inset (A Root); 25U (J & D Bartlett); 26BR (J Foott); 47C (A Root); 48U (C Willock); 49U (D & M Plage); 51B (J & D Bartlett); 57U (B Davidson); 60U (J & D Bartlett); 68U (J Foott); 96U (J & D Bartlett); 96B (J & D Bartlett); 98U (J Foott); 103B (T & L Bomford); 106 (D Plage); 120B (M Linley); 123BR (J Foott); 128UR (M Linley); 130U (A Root); 131U (J & D Bartlett); 138 (C Buxton/A Price); 141BR (A Root).